THE

Official

Guide

to

Christmas

IN THE

South

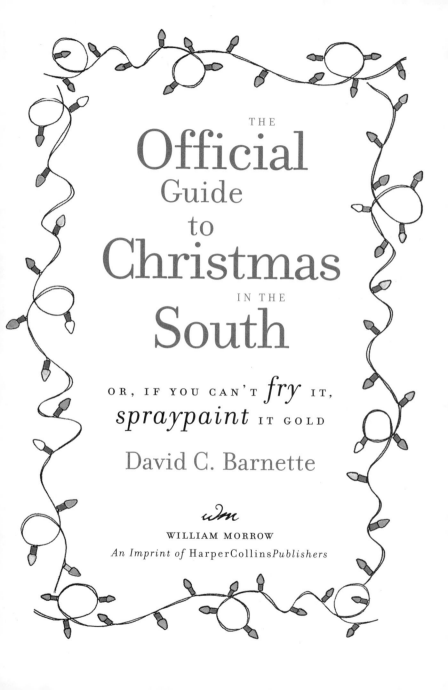

THE

Official
Guide
to
Christmas
IN THE
South

OR, IF YOU CAN'T *fry* IT,
spraypaint IT GOLD

David C. Barnette

𝔚𝔪

WILLIAM MORROW
An Imprint of HarperCollins*Publishers*

This book contains advice about the most important day in the South. Said advice is not intended to replace Junior League membership. All efforts have been made to assure the accuracy of the information in this book; however, most of these efforts were made north of the Mason-Dixon line and should be politely dismissed. The publisher and author disclaim liability for any incidents involving elevated cholesterol levels, aerosol intake, or rolling blackouts due to excessive use of Christmas lights.

A trade paperback edition of this book was originally published in 2004 by MDi Publishing and illustrated by Timothy Dozier.

THE OFFICIAL GUIDE TO CHRISTMAS IN THE SOUTH. Copyright © 2004 by MDi Publishing. All rights reserved. Printed in the United States of America. No part of this book may be used or reproduced in any manner whatsoever without written permission except in the case of brief quotations embodied in critical articles and reviews. For information address HarperCollins Publishers, 10 East 53rd Street, New York, NY 10022.

HarperCollins books may be purchased for educational, business, or sales promotional use. For information please write: Special Markets Department, HarperCollins Publishers, 10 East 53rd Street, New York, NY 10022.

FIRST EDITION

Designed by Chris Welch
Illustrations by Donna Mehalko

Printed on acid-free paper

Library of Congress Cataloging-in-Publication Data has been applied for.

ISBN-13: 978-0-06-085053-1
ISBN-10: 0-06-085053-1

05 06 07 08 09 ❖/RRD 10 9 8 7 6 5 4 3 2 1

To Ashley, Cailey, and Sibley: the merriest

Contents

THE

Official
Guide
to
Christmas
IN THE
South

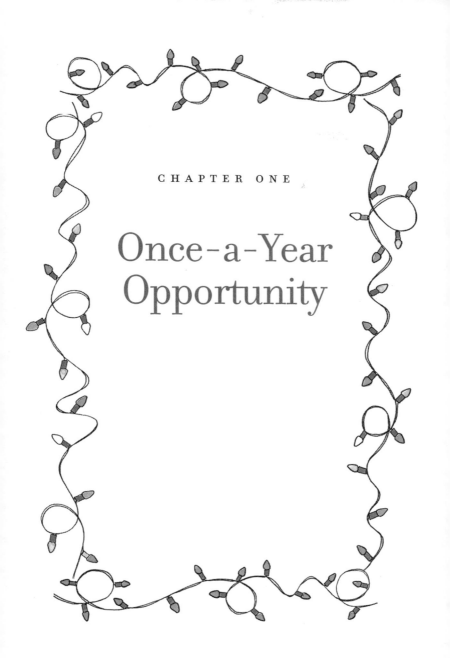

CHAPTER ONE

Once-a-Year
Opportunity

The national media portrays the South, impossibly, as the Mecca of both religion and a good party. For once, the national media is right. But there's more to it than what we see on TV: the Bush twins stumbling out of Austin bars, the Ten Commandments hauled into a state capitol on a front-end loader. What the media should focus on more is that one special time of year when the divine and debutantes all take center stage in a perfect storm of hot glue and cheese grits: Christmas.

There are certain social needs that can

only be met at this special time . . .

*A*dvertising the family name. This is the only time of year when five bucks and a poinsettia can get the family name in the church bulletin. Atlanta ad agencies have rarely landed such a captive audience.

Promoting the family image. From January to Thanksgiving, only real estate agents, attorneys, and hookers can freely distribute photos of themselves. Christmas, however, is open season for the mass mailing of family photos.

*S*howing off the house. One of the more bizarre things about life in the South is how a dinner inevitably leads to a tour of the house. This is equally true of antebellum and double-wide homes, each of which have notable features to be highlighted. This is the time of year to show it all off, whether of the garden-district or garden-tub variety.

Exercising the silver. While Northerners sing about silver bells, Southerners are rigging their kitchen sinks with baking soda and aluminum foil in experimental attempts to clean the sheer volume of silver necessities. The resulting acrid smell has been compared to that of a home perm, and is often masked with the use of potpourri Crockpots.

The fact that all of this happens only once a year is why a little advance planning takes place. Fortunes of cotton and tobacco weren't built overnight, and a noteworthy Christmas isn't planned over Thanksgiving turkey.

January

One last party and home tour. Christmas doesn't officially end until Epiphany. Bargains, however, end around January 2. Call mortgage company and ask to skip January payment. Invest proceeds in marked-down holiday wrapping goods and ornaments.

February

Only Mardi Gras is as tacky as Christmas. While spraypainting wingtip shoes gold to wear on a Mardi Gras float, get a jump start on spraying holiday goods.

May

Multitask. While searching the drawers for Teacher Appreciation Week gifts, separate random gifts by price categories. Create separate drawers or baskets for each price tier and stock with appropriately sized gift bags.

June

Reuse extra annual silver-bell ornaments as gifts for the bride and groom. Call jeweler to reserve upcoming bell coordinated with silver pattern.

September

Purchase fifth of Maker's Mark. Drive out to Christmas tree farm and ignore the sign warning that no trees may be tagged or reserved. Give fifth to tree farmer and nail aluminum nameplate into trunk of favorite tree.

October

Lay electrical infrastructure for holiday lawn decoration, then disguise by setting up halfhearted Halloween displays. Most types of grass will recover from buried cables by mid-November.

March

In preparation for both wedding and holiday seasons, restock favorite stores with signed calling cards.

April

Last call for rosy-cheeked portrait of family skiing. Consult *Women's Wear Daily* to project what will be in style eight months from now.

July

Wedding season is over, so good photographers are looking for work. Schedule sessions for more formal photographs or other original artwork for this year's Christmas card if ski sweater looked too bulky. Summer vacation pictures from theme parks are also acceptable. Remember to take off fanny pack.

August

Send children to school (boarding if possible) in order to prepare in earnest.

November

Begin untangling lights, fastening hooks to ornaments, and checking for breakage. All wrapping for nonfamily should be completed. Serve turkey and dressing to family as a test run for holiday china and crystal. Note any cracks or chips. Keep Replacements Unlimited on speed dial.

December

Confirm standing appointments with psychiatrist, florist, and AA.

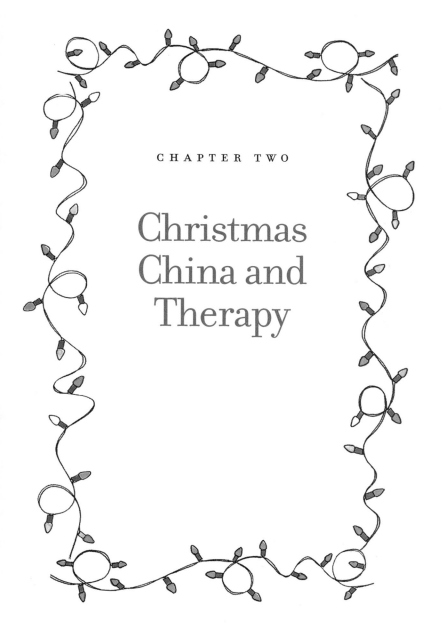

CHAPTER TWO

Christmas
China and
Therapy

New Yorkers pay feng shui consultants to ferret out their fortunes from prosperity corners and to rid their hallways of negative energies. Southerners, meanwhile, keep the heavy symbolism and fortunes in the china cabinet. Christmas china comes off the shelf up to one week prior to Thanksgiving and is stored without spots on the night of Epiphany. No exceptions.

There are two kinds of Christmas china: special and everyday. People from places like New York might call "everyday Christmas china" an oxymoron. We might call people who hang dream catchers in their prosperity corners oxymorons, too.

Anyone claiming to have special
Christmas china should be subjected to
unannounced raids.

Truly special Christmas china will only be found in one of three places: in the main china hutch, on the table on December 25, or passing through the sink one at a time with acres of plush towels nearby.

Special Christmas china will be marked Spode, Mottahedeh, Royal Crown Derby, Royal Worcester, or Wedgwood. Inspectors should find the china, if stored, with paper towels as buffers to prevent scratching. Yankee mailorder catalogs offer quilted china buffers for this purpose. These items are bulky, often sport mushroom motifs, and aren't even worthy of covering up the toaster at the beach house.

Everyday china includes literally
thousands of potential disasters licensed
by everyone from Dansk to Disney.

I t's not that there is any problem with everyday holiday china; the problem lies in the cheesy Christmas scenes that involve nutcrackers, morbidly obese wildlife, and Santa's visit to Bethlehem. These vignettes are only useful at over-the-top themed Dirty Santa parties where the liquor flows as fast as the catty comments.

Don't discount the paper patterns with matching paper napkins (not really paper—made, rather, from a blended foam mixture in great selection at Winn Dixie and Publix). These are to be used for family-only leftover dinners or for sending cookies to public school teachers. Some people gently rinse the plates for reuse, but this is not recommended for those with compromised immune systems.

Any woman who has done a Ritz
weekend in Atlanta just to find a basic
black dress understands wardrobing.
Wardrobing of china is a hot trend for
new brides and seasoned
entertainers alike.

A few simple rules apply when wardrobing:

1. You must currently own a nonholiday china pattern in bone or white.
2. All five pieces of the pattern must be in your inventory: plate, salad, bread, cup and saucer (rim soup is accepted to replace bread plate if necessary; pots de crème are completely unnecessary and worth every dollar).
3. As the new national conglomerate banks do not specialize in china loans, tap into home equity for the finest holiday pattern you can afford.
4. Make sure your holiday and regular china patterns have the same background. It is not acceptable to purchase a bone holiday pattern to mix with a white pattern. If divorce, remarriage or late-season hurricanes ever create such an ungodly combination, the only respectable solution is to buy white linen napkins and have them monogrammed loudly in bone.

After determining your china combinations, purchase the salad plate or rim soup of the holiday pattern and place atop the dinner plate of your fine china. Example: Royal Crown Derby's Carlton Gold dinner plate topped with Spode's Christmas Rose salad. So beautiful, some hostesses prefer not to cover the plates with food and simply to serve cigarettes and liquor.

THE I CHING OF CHRISTMAS CHINA

You don't need to read tea leaves to tell fortunes; just look at the cup.

Lenox Holiday: You like safety and are likely to build straight from a *Southern Living* floor plan. You may be either a grandmother bequeathing this to the next generation or the next generation filling in grandmother's missing pieces. Be careful on eBay.

Lenox Winter Greetings: Bulky birds on china indicate a life of excess. Buying in bulk is one thing; eating and drinking in bulk is another. Stay away from big-bag chips and boxed wine, and remember: Gaudí was an architect; gaudy is a choice.

Spode Christmas Tree: Your mother will forgive you for that rebellious phase when you dropped the *h* at the end of Sarah, but she will always call you by your double name: Sarah Frances, Sarah Katherine, etc.

Spode Disney Christmas Tree: There is concern that Michael Eisner may have held Spode hostage. The evil behind this pattern will take over your life. First, the china. Next, you invest in the Disney Vacation Club. Turn off *Finding Nemo* in the den and stop shopping online. Your children need you.

Spode Christmas Rose: You only meant to wardrobe. But the salad plate led to the rim soup and now you have the whole set. While taking this summer's college tour with the children, look in boutiques for matching accessories.

Johnson Brothers: Sisters favor the Brothers. Usually twins with rhyming names and/or sorority sisters from second- or third-tier sororities (based on the Ole Miss Sorority Scale). Great price point makes it understandable that you bought party quantities. Plus, you got a great interest rate on that credit card.

Fitz and Floyd St. Nicholas: Holiday china should say Merry Christmas, not Married Up. Consider chipping and/or crackling a few pieces to give St. Newmoney a patina, then redeem yourself by upping your pledge to the opera this year.

Gail Pittman Pottery: Hats off to you for branching out and making the holidays more casual. You were the first in the neighborhood to serve balsamic vinegar, and people love your artisan breads. Your watercolor efforts are bound to pay off soon.

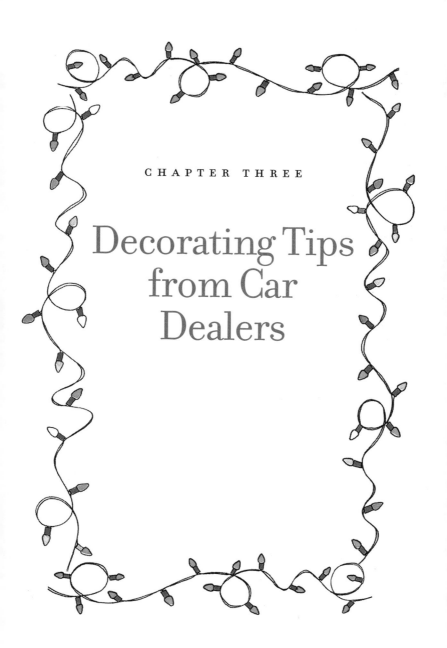

CHAPTER THREE

Decorating Tips from Car Dealers

One of the biggest mistakes Yankees make is considering the house when decorating the yard. Winter wonderlands are all about the car. Yes, holiday spotlights flooding in through the windows will keep your kids up late at night, but the goal here isn't Silent Night. It's curb appeal. And nobody knows curb appeal like a used car dealer. Following are car-lot tips from a Southeastern car dealers' association handbook. They can transform your lawn. And your life.

Learn from car dealers, who learned from Bourbon Street dancers: Stop a crowd with movement.

Auto dealers put the newest model up on a spinny thing, then rent one of those hot-air figures to stand and wave over the building—do you think they would sell many cars if all they did was put a spray of glass cranberries around the door? You can introduce movement to your Christmas lawn *and* maintain good taste thanks to mechanical grapevine animals. Yes, those favorite white-light beasts of visual burden began to move a few years ago, and they're still a traffic-stopper. Just be careful not to place them together; as noses rise and rears fall, you don't want your deer to appear to be engaging in unsavory acts.

Learn from Joseph, Santa, and
Dolly Parton: Cash in on color.

W hen did it become a rule that only white lights are in good taste? Imagine a parking lot full of white-only autos. No, you'll best sell your holiday theme if you execute it in full color. Fully cover all Bradford pears and other specimen trees, then outline good architectural features. Just remember to remove the flasher bulb.

Bait and switch. Santa has to keep his promises; you don't. There's nothing wrong with using licensed characters by the roadside to attract families, then offering your own tasteful concoctions of colored lights and pineapples behind the hedgerow.

Turn up the heat.

Hot deals attract a crowd. So does the heat of one million bulbs. One Southern lawn featured thousands of colored bulbs on each of hundreds of sprawling live oaks. In the December fog, a pilot flying overhead reported it as a forest fire. *That's* the Christmas spirit.

Christmas is no time to go for Yard of the Month honors. The measure of a well-decorated Christmas lawn is a visit from the police regarding traffic delays in front of your home.

Many people rely on new traffic, but one of the most efficient methods is to build traffic through slowdowns and/or handouts. Don't rely on the old-fashioned tradition of having grandpa dressed up on the porch as Santa with a bag of candy. Most children today can't be peeled from the newest DVD playing in the backseat. To slow the line of traffic, place HoHo curbside with instructions to engage the entire car in conversation while a montage of holiday movie trailers is queued up for a lawn show. Many homes have caught on to 1980s projection technology to create fascinating swirling snowflakes and other motifs on the garage door. This will not slow traffic. But a wide-screen plasma TV in an open garage, with surround sound extension-corded to the curb? That's a showstopper.

How did women end up in the fray of lawn decorating? Didn't it used to be the domain of Chevy Chase and staple-gun-wielding fathers?

S ome men blame the loss of territory on home superstores that have catered to women with luxuries such as wide aisles and lighting. Others are all too happy staying in and watching football to complain about not decorating the lawn. In truth, women received lawn suffrage through the SUV. Somewhere in Chattanooga, one nameless Junior Leaguer crossed the line. As if decorating the interior of the house weren't enough, she lashed an extra wreath to the grille of her husband's Expedition. A trend followed. A cousin in Macon took the idea and ran with it. An aunt in Opelika followed suit. Soon, women had officially taken over outdoor decorating—and grapevine animals came to life.

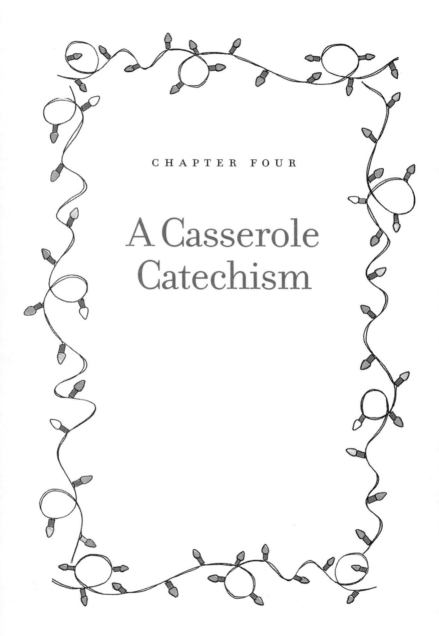

CHAPTER FOUR

A Casserole
Catechism

Of all the mysteries in the Bible, the greatest is: Why didn't the three Wise Men bring Mary a casserole?

No one knows the answer, but it's clear that the Wise Men wouldn't be a big hit running around the South delivering myrrh. Mary may have been charmed by the Wise Men's gift of aromatic resin, but those were also the days before plug-in devices cranked out cinnamon and clove 24/7.

Today the Wise trio would take one look at the bright star in the sky and go in search of a casserole.

Southerners, known for baking cobblers by the square yard, have no shortage of cookware, recipes, and caterers to meet any casserole need. Just as important as the foodstuff itself, though, is its mode of delivery.

Pyrex in sterling stand: Pretentious (thus perfect). Tip: Dress down by writing name and number in blue ballpoint on masking tape, applied to the bottom.

Pyrex in silverplate: Tip: Cover word "silverplate" with engraved calling card, adding phone number in black ink. Apply with superglue.

Pyrex in hot/cold zippered carrier: Sporty, fun, and young. Excellent when attempting to be invited into a coveted supper/running club.

Pyrex with a pot holder and plastic wrap: Only at church. Use holiday colors. Must be holiday-themed aluminum, or they'll assume the casserole was your frozen standby for funerals.

Holidays are for celebrating the ties that bind. And nothing binds quite like cream of chicken and Velveeta.

Once the appropriate vessel has been chosen, casseroles may be made, preferably en masse. Of all the known cooking techniques, Henry Ford's assembly line is most relevant. The vehicle, in fact, is a kitchen tool used more than once by Southern women who need to crush saltines and/or pecans to top a dozen casseroles at a time. Another handy kitchen casserole appliance is the cell phone, which allows casseroles to be gathered, gift-tagged, and charged to the credit card at a favorite caterer while waiting in the carpool line.

Whether homemade or catered, the casserole is no longer a stand-alone item; it would be like giving a child one Christmas present and no stocking. Instead, consider some of these casserole stuffers.

1. Keep casserole warm with an oven brick wrapped in a piqué towel with the recipient's single monogram on it (it's imperative to maintain the full alphabet in monogrammed items at any rate).

2. Wrap bread in a subtle toile-patterned dish towel. Tie with ribbon.

3. Make concentrated sweet tea and deliver in quart jar dressed up with a monogrammed cocktail napkin skirted beneath the ring.

A most inappropriate accompaniment to a casserole is your own company. Just because the recipient insists that you stay and eat with them doesn't mean they really feel that way—and certainly doesn't imply they want to share their liquor.

inally, a note on conservation. Just as peak demand for electricity has caused rolling blackouts in major cities, the Southern Casserole Grid has shut down before due to the combination of Christmas, winter deaths, and elective surgeries. Clearly, none of the three can be reasonably avoided. There is only one way to solve the issue of global casserole warming: Create a regifting section in your freezer.

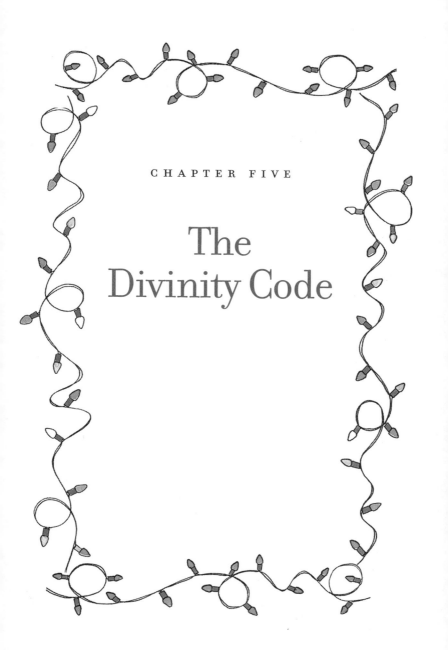

CHAPTER FIVE

The
Divinity Code

Thank-you notes will be graded and thanking someone for Mexican wedding cookies when they gave you divinity earns an F.

When sitting down to write Christmas thank-you notes (on, say, Thanksgiving after-noon), certain standards are expected.

1. You will write in black ink (with the exception of real squid ink for some older zip codes and gold gel pen in some newer).

2. You will address the envelope formally, even if hand-delivered to your sister.

3. You will name items properly.

In the Southern thank-you note, gratitude is measured in specificity. This isn't typically so hard until one begins writing, and continues writing for days, thank-you notes for tins of sweets. Oh, the tins of sweets.

It is probably perfectly acceptable
outside of the South to jot down in blue
ballpoint, "Sally, thanks so much for
the chocolate-caramel thingies!"

Unfortunately, this does not earn a good new year in this region, where that note would translate roughly into, "Sally, we ate your candy but won't require your playdates in the future." No, you will kindly look into the tin of fate and discern between Southern colonels and fiddlesticks.

Victorians became obsessed with the secret language of flowers (phlox, for instance, means "our hearts are united," and cedar means "I live for thee"). Southerners in general have avoided such symbolism and consider it a good thing anytime flowers survive the heat. Moreover, phlox is ugly and cedar bouquets are about as well received as a tourniquet.

Secret messages here are tapped out in another code entirely: One of sugar, pecans, chocolate chips, and margarine.

Translating the morsel code

Fiddlesticks: This is a feisty gift, a highbrow touché. No one can turn down the combination of pecans, chocolate, and caramel, but the name and the fact that this is a dessert cut into bars can convey a lighthearted jab. Perfect for that neighbor whose fence is six inches onto your property.

Southern colonels: You are admired. A flattering gift from family to family. If the gift is from a single man or woman, spouse beware.

Polliwogs: This one is about being cute. Lovely when directed to the children. When directed to adults, usually is an attempt to get into a renowned-for-fun supper club.

Tiger paws: After some of the recent accidents involving animal trainers and zookeepers, this is about as cheerful as sending someone a chocolate scythe. Candy senders must stay up on current events.

Bark: A studious gift. Often is associated with a plea to join a book club, the good kind with food and booze. Whether the bark is pecan-chocolate, peppermint-chocolate, or any other combination matters little. Start watching C-SPAN *Booknotes*.

Fudge: From the heart. Often an overweight heart. Sometimes a bless-her-heart. But nothing warms the old ticker like a slab of well-greased fudge.

Baklava: A studious gift. Often is associated with an invitation to join a book club, the horrible kind, perhaps a Great Books study in a house that smells of mothballs and garlic. Baklava givers also tend to be active in arts fundraisers. Enjoy the honey and get out your checkbook.

Praline: Marking of territory. Pralines are the trump card of Southern candies. They can be as dreadful and bland as an old calling card, but clearly someone is reminding you that they're more Southern. One-up them in a few months with a King Cake from New Orleans.

Heavenly hash: Once the exclusive domain of nuns and housekeepers, heavenly hash has become a household favorite. Domestic and divine undertones are no longer interpreted here, but the light marshmallow bulk may indicate an eating disorder. Consider an intervention for January.

Divinity: What, pray tell, is divine about a candy that tastes like nothing but egg and sugar and can only be made under the rarest of climate conditions? No one really knows, but it remains one of the ultimate candy gifts. Topped with whole pecans? You're the best. Topped with pieces of pecan halves? Bad market. Mixed with crumbled pecans, à la cookies and cream? The giver is a Yankee.

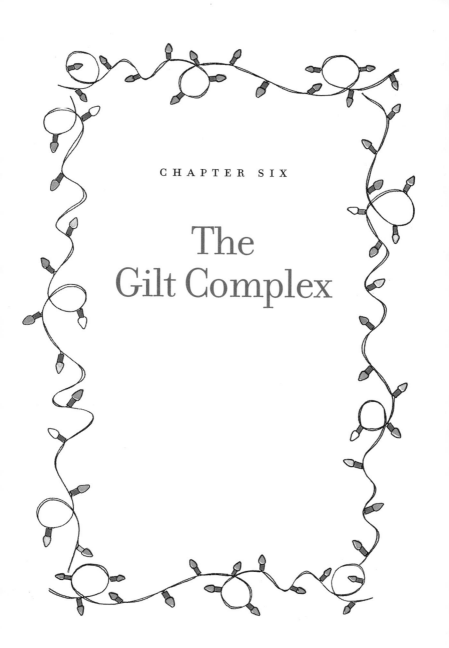

CHAPTER SIX

The
Gilt Complex

The only place busier than the North Pole during the holidays is the shrink's office. Therapists generally don't accept new patients or see their families between Thanksgiving and Epiphany. While these doctors may be good at helping with the guilt complex, they're of little help when it's time for the gilt complex.

THE ANCIENT ART OF GILDING

For thousands of years, gold has been formed into brittle leaves delicately applied by skilled artisans to achieve subtle accents of gold. Subtlety and gold aren't such good bedfellows below the Mason-Dixon line, where gold comes with a spray nozzle. What aerosol did for hair was nothing compared to what it's contributed to Christmas. Gold-painted trimmings have become the high hair of seasonal festivities.

Guidelines

and paint lines

Many a newcomer has asked, "What can be spraypainted gold?" The answer is anything that can't give you a gift or be deep-fried.

Spoiled fruit is a perennial favorite (sometimes literally, as oranges shrink little from year to year). Pineapples, once a simple sign of Southern hospitality, need only thirty seconds under the nozzle to be worthy of Graceland. Magnolia leaves go from green to gaudy. Even plastic Santas, faded from years of El Niño, become magical again with a Midas glaze. A new and sculptural trend is to spraypaint extra caramel-crusted gourmet apples. Apply a liberal coating of gold and attach a golden angel to the top of the stick with hot glue. Two anchor a mantle; three make a display worthy of a Fairmont lobby. A lone golden apple makes an excellent gift for mailman or substitute teacher.

It is better to give than to receive, but it is better to gild than to deal with the whole gift issue.

Southerners don't stop at giving gifts to family, friends, neighbors, and random acquaintances. Nearly everyone who comes into contact with you, your family, or your garbage expects a gift. It's these holiday guilt complexes—who gets which value of gift—that tip many borderline personality disorders into veritable covered-dish dinners of dysfunction.

Here's a quick guide to who gets what:

Postman: You could just give him McDonald's gift certificates. But this is the person responsible for your catalogs and checks. He or she also makes sure neighbors don't accidentally see your bankruptcy papers. Call Omaha Steaks.

Hairdresser: Honestly, it makes you miss the days of Kutz-n-Kurlz in the trailer. As hairdressers all turn more spalike, the gift ante gets raised. Visit RedEnvelope.com.

Caddy/Pro: It's unfortunate that people stereotype caddies and tennis pros as always having and/or knowing about affairs. It's even more unfortunate that the stereotype tends to be accurate. Cash is appropriate. And in large sums. This is hush money.

Pharmacist: Such a key person in your life, but one you surely know little about. Pharmacists get very little pampering in their lives. Excellent candidates for bath baskets, extra loofah, etc.

Plumber: He's seen inside your medicine cabinets and under the sink. You already know the number to Omaha Steaks.

Minister: Tough one. Does a generous gift make up for the fact that you don't tithe, or simply underscore the fact that you do have the means to give? Answer: Count the minister's gift as part of your tithe. Two-night stays at nearby resorts are good. They hate religious books and gift certificates to religious stores. That's like giving lard to a fry cook.

Schoolteacher: Two of the most dangerous dens of iniquity are the boardroom at the Junior League and the teachers' lounge. Don't let the apples and smiley faces fool you. They compare gifts. Make it good. You're not going to be graded on a curve here.

CHAPTER SEVEN

Inside
Christmas

Tara-like columns are a cliché. Architects in the South can tell you that clients are far too practical and rooted these days for such plantation whimsies. Today's Southern house is designed around two far more casual everyday needs: a staircase suitable for portrait photography, and a Christmas tree spot worthy of a magazine spread.

Children often bring home adorable handcrafted ornaments. They should by all means be allowed to decorate a tree with these heartfelt crafts—Christmas is, after all, for children. This quaint tree should then be moved to the back, back sunroom. The publicly viewed Christmas tree spot is reserved for the real tree. This public tree, architects take note, must:

1. Be visible from the street—preferably through beveled glass.
2. Be visible from the dining room—preferably through beveled glass.
3. Sit under the highest ceilings in the house.
4. Not block French doors to barbecue.
5. Be wired to a separate breaker.

Beyond the Tree:

Bugs and Boughs

Northern magazines are full of beautiful ideas involving stringing one's house with unwrapped candy canes, popcorn, and cranberries. These people have apparently never seen how many palmetto bugs (known elsewhere as "roaches") can fit on one candy cane. Such concoctions also invariably send signals to fire-ant colonies. In our climate, one is better served to string the tree with more unappetizing items. Should it be necessary to decorate with edibles, also make ornaments by applying gold spray paint to roach motels. Hang deep in tree. To avoid ants, set up numerous Christmas villages out of reach of children and sprinkle liberally with a snow made of powdered sugar and boric acid.

CALLER ID IS THE NEW CAROLING

I n days of old, Southerners gathered before porches to carol in the holidays. Unfortunately, this is now impossible due to the prohibitive number of Suburbans involved. Instead, caroling by phone has become de rigueur. Figgy pudding has been replaced by call waiting, and the old embarrassing listen-at-the-door scenario is now handled by voice mail. Cold? Yes, but with a distinct advantage. Not only can one screen out undesirables, but caller ID leaves proof of big-name visits in much the way calling cards used to. Whereas big-name calling cards were once left out in the foyer for others to see (and, frankly, big-name cards were sometimes printed by social climbers with connections to unscrupulous local engravers), the caller ID box requires scrolling through numbers. Fortunately, The Sharper Image now offers a projection-style caller ID device that allows good family names to fly about the kitchen wall like wind-driven snow.

Your Mantra?

Mind over Mantel

Many a visitor has asked why homes in such tropical climates have some of the most elaborate fireplaces in the nation. The answer is simple: Have you ever tried draping holiday decorations on a window unit? Mantel decoration is meant to be a simple joy, and shouldn't put fear into young couples as it often does. Only a few minor rules must be observed:

1. All mantel decorations must coordinate with year-round over-mantel art.
2. Over-mantel art may not be removed. This is called cheating.
3. Symmetry must be either wildly violated or respected to the millimeter. Buckingham Palace staffers have excellent table-setting templates that can be valuable tools here.
4. Christmas cards are acceptable only when:
   a. arranged by desirability of zip code
   b. cohesive in theme
   c. used to hide electrical sources and bundles of soggy paper towels used to keep greenery fresh.
5. Christmas villages may not be used as mantel décor. This is called cheating.

THERE'S A NEW BREED OF VILLAGE PEOPLE

The increasing popularity of Christmas villages presents a definite problem in this addiction-prone region. Yes, in a civilization where rehab is considered a spa treatment, the notion of a lighted ceramic holiday village can quickly turn into an act of playing God. How to know when you're out of control? Simple. Just ask yourself these Christmas village questions:

1. Does my Christmas village stand in the way of relationships with real people?
2. Have I ever cut Styrofoam to form mountains?
3. Does my Christmas village train appear to be performing a genuine economic role?
4. Do some of my villagers own more than one vehicle?
5. Have fast-food restaurants begun to compete in my Christmas village?
6. Does my village have access to and/or a need for emergency medical service?

If your village has gotten out of control, don't overreact and destroy it. Simply place excessive village homes and businesses in their original boxes, wrap, and regift.

Holiday Hideaway

Now that you are ready to decorate, it's time to hide the every-day accessories or theme them into your holiday program. Below are suggested solutions:

Item	Solution
Waterford clock	Drape with holly and ivy. Or place in mom's lingerie drawer. Toward the back, where the sexy stuff is.
Wedgwood ashtray	Lock it up in the gun cabinet. Note: While pheasant feathers and other hunting themes are in vogue, it is never appropriate to use red-and-white ribbon to "candy stripe" rifles.
Glass paperweight	Wrap in nonholiday dish towel and place in cachepot.
Cachepot	Wrap in nonholiday dish towel and place in large basket.
Large basket	Place, along with all other difficult-to-place and bulky nonholiday items, in children's rooms. Christmas isn't about kids. It's about décor.
Staffordshire dogs	Dad's underwear drawer. Near old athletic supporter. Don't look back.

CHAPTER EIGHT

Gifts That Keep Regiving

If you don't believe in reincarnation,
follow a gift bag around this Christmas.

When Scarlett O'Hara came down the stairs wearing drapes, she established the South's reign over recycling. While Northerners make a big fuss over bottle tops and crushed cans, people below the Mason-Dixon are sparing landfills from the wasteful mass of pointless gifts.

Certain categories of gifts are prime for regifting, that act by which gifts spread across the region faster than kudzu.

The gifts generally need to be highly impersonal, durably packaged, and commodity-priced.

Each gift has a logical place in the regifting food chain:

Item	From	Pass on to
Cube calendars	Coworkers	Spouse's coworkers
Inspirational books	Overzealous church members	Maid
Gift mugs	Spouse's coworkers	Secondary-subject teachers
Bath/fragrance sets	Friends who are teachers	Mail carrier
Isotoner gloves	Grandmothers with memory loss	Grandmothers with memory loss
Wine in velvet bag	Supper club members	Hairdresser
Southern Living subscription	Parents	Sorority sisters who have moved to states that begin with an *I*.

Ultimately, the month of December becomes an extended game of Dirty Santa, with everyone scrambling to pass on the worst gifts.

The goal is to end up with the lowest number of mugs and the highest milligramage of wine in velvet bags. (Exception: Sadly, teachers inevitably come home with boxes of mugs each Christmas, and the goal for them is a successful yard sale or an exaggerated tax write-off.) A note of caution: This scheme is also like playing the Six Degrees of Kevin Bacon. There's a significant risk of regifting the original giver. Solution? Keeping records of the transaction is a lost cause—unless you have access to UPS tracking software. Instead, just keep trendy and otherwise noticeable gifts out of the recycling food chain. Send these gifts—like plaster "hear no evil, see no evil, speak no evil" monkey sets—north of the Mason-Dixon line. Better yet, dig out the address for that '92 exchange student you hosted from Slovenia.

Don't throw the
proof out with the bath water

Regifting can save thousands of dollars, but the cost can also be high if one is busted for having passed on a gift. Whenever possible, stockpile digital photos of gifts being used in your home: one shot, for instance, could feature a family member relaxing next to a side table with a steaming gift mug of coffee next to an open inspirational book. Rather than producing this evidence when accused of regifting, consider framing several of these photos in an inexpensive collage frame and displaying at home and office. It's also critical to never throw away receipts or store-name boxes and gift bags. These lend authenticity to your regifting efforts—and increase the odds of racking up in-store credits.

Never mix Dirty Santa with

Dirty Dancing

Every game has its danger zone. In regifting, there's one place you don't want to go: the dance teacher. Maybe your kids tumble. Maybe they're in ballet, tap, or jazz. But just as you admire that leg-warmer-wearing woman for her ability to coordinate thirty pudgy children into a flowery waltz, she's also able to keep track of the gifts being juggled through her studio. Think you're going to pass along a Kate Spade knockoff or fake Burberry umbrella on Miss Susan? Chances are she'll bust you—especially if you're a slow payer.

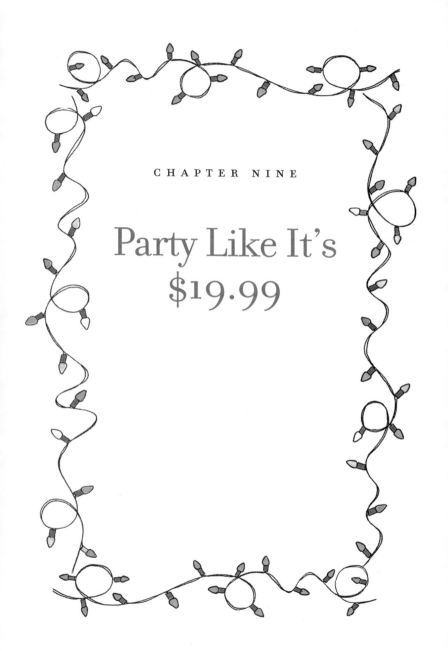

CHAPTER NINE

Party Like It's $19.99

Take one spiral-cut ham. Add fifty white paper lunch bags filled with sand and candles. What you have is a carnivorous fire hazard otherwise known as the Southern Christmas party.

In days of old, plantations were designed with large windows so that orchestras could play on the veranda, thus adding live music without blocking the buffet line. Today's version may involve a Bose Wave radio and open sliding-glass doors, but the scale remains just as overdone.

Unplug the smoke alarm

Fire and safety officials recommend replacing smoke alarm batteries when changing clocks for daylight saving time. Southerners find it more convenient to do this the morning after a Christmas party, for which the alarm was at some point removed and/or beaten with a stick. With cigars, grosses of candles, and little cans of Sterno heating silver trays of cheese grits, the party can easily produce more smoke than a KISS concert.

WHAT NOT TO WEAR

Maybe it's the fact that outfits are bound to come home smelling so smoky they should be thrown away. Maybe it's the fact that the lighting is so bad, outfits have to be exceptionally tacky to be seen. Whatever the reason, Christmas party attire tends to surpass Mardi Gras in sheer tackiness—and conversation starters.

If they're wearing	Then break the ice by saying
Lightbulb jewelry	Bet you're enjoying Christmas vacation!
Christmas tree tie	Can you believe how low interest rates are?
Grinch tie	So what's a four-bedroom running in this part of town?
Oversize Christmas sweater	Have you been to the new Atlanta Bread Company?
Santa hat accented with mistletoe	I'm married.

Sounds of the Season

J ust as the party begins with good liquor and winds down with runs to the convenience store, music changes throughout the life of the party. Yes, the South used to be known for parties with gay waltzes, but the key word there is "gay," and waltzes were only popular prior to the advent of David Allan Coe.

Sometimes parties begin with an attempt at elegance. Digital technology has made it possible to bore guests with the sounds of local symphonic and operatic performers. This sort of CD generally won't reach the eighth track before someone puts in Jimmy Buffett's "Christmas Island" or the Dixie Chicks' "Merry Christmas from the Family." By the end of the party, guests are often eating aerosol cheese and listening to its musical equivalent.

Y'all get in line

I t's no accident that Western Sizzlin does so well in our region. The appeal of grabbing a plate and bellying up to the trough is tough to beat. *Southern Living* sets a standard each year for candlelit buffets where each guest is met by a personalized-ornament napkin ring. Seductive though they may be, these buffet plans with "make-ahead" tips can be as tough to accomplish as the annual *Southern Living* cover cake.

In the end, the old standby menus work best:

1. *Anything in a pie crust:* It's not just for pecans anymore. Mini crusts can be balanced on Christmas napkins and provide a full meal of mini quiches, mini shrimp cocktails, gumbo baskets, and mini pecan pies. Ambitious Southern cooks have taken it to the next level and lined up all their mini pies assembly-line style, giving them a quick Cajun injection and a dip in the Fry Daddy.

2. *Bambi:* Always a big hit, venison is especially popular at holiday parties. Venison gumbo, venison chili, and shredded venison barbecue can all be ladled into mini pie shells. Wives who are embarrassed at serving so much venison sometimes try to compensate with witty calligraphy menu cards reading the likes of "Reindeer Chili."

3. *Marinated shrimp:* As much as a month ahead of time, refrigerators in the South begin to look like the laboratories of mad scientists. Enormous jars are filled with shrimp and a pickling concoction that becomes more bizarre as the party approaches. Mustard seeds, Dale's steak sauce, expired orange juice, and wormy tequila are favored marinades.

4. *Ham:* Vegetarians best look the other way. As long as there are funerals and Christmas, pigs will be giving their lives to the spiral-cut cause. Much like handing a box of raisins to a whiny child, large hams meet a buffet's quantity needs while requiring very little effort. No one bakes their own hams anymore, though everyone claims to. Instead, precooked hams are purchased and then personalized with last-minute glazes of Coca-Cola, brown sugar, sorghum, and leftover salsa. Hams are often then violated with whole pecans prior to being Cajun-injected and deep-fried.

CHAPTER TEN

'Twas the night

It has been said that hunting season

saves marriages. . . .

L ong winter weeks apart are sometimes required for a couple to recover from those frantic dark hours before the children awake on Christmas morning. Window dressers at Tiffany don't know the rigor and pressure of a three-year-old belle's Christmas morning expectations. While the Northern version of Papa Noel may be satisfied leaving a couchful of toys that require assembly, Southern children would be emotionally wrecked by a doll or stuffed animal with an empty body cavity where batteries should be.

Isn't she a doll?

New dolls arrive from the factory in a horror of plastic, rigor mortis, and bad hair. Men who have begged out of brushing their own daughters' hair for the past 364 days are suddenly enlisted into the duty of coiffing and dressing dolls. The job begins on a manly note, as releasing a Barbie or American Girl from her packaging requires pliers and electrician certification. By the early hours of morning, however, men find themselves fluffing the collars of colonial blouses and testing the capability of dolls to perform their advertised function, whether that be candle-dipping, Vespa-riding, baking, or urination.

MRS. GOODWRENCH

Mothers, on the other hand, have little time to spend catering to dolls' needs as it is their time-honored duty to assemble all wagons and bicycles so as to avoid loud cursing or shoddy and unsafe assembly.

I believe the children are our future

Somewhere just before dawn, husbands and wives are heard screaming "We aren't doing this for us, honey, we're doing it for the children." Unfortunately, they're not talking about the Christmas preparations. It's the marriage. Christmas Eve is the night when therapists unplug their phones and divorce attorneys hire extra help. Fortunately, light-sleeping children assume they're hearing the ruckus of reindeer on the roof; many a child's memory of glimpsing Rudolph can be attributed to the flashing lights of emergency personnel.

Before the sun comes up, however, the tension lowers, the milk and cookies are consumed, and, when necessary, bail is posted. Children then awaken to the Christmas morning of their parents' dreams.

Pomp and Circumstantial Evidence

Because most Southern homes are designed for at least one grand entrance, children are typically filmed and flash-photographed in a procession down a staircase or highly decorated hall. The paparazzi-like strobe of photography indicates not so much an interest in the children as an effort by one spouse to daze them while the other spouse, newly alert on coffee, picks up telltale shreds of Styrofoam packaging.

Gifts are arranged to be discovered in a parade-like procession. Small fans are sometimes rigged up to swirl handlebar streamers; rounding the corner to the sofa, children come upon alarmingly detailed model railroad villages and colonial scenes staffed by American Girl dolls. Small recreational vehicles await with doors open and keys in the ignition, while larger three- and four-wheelers are hidden behind azalea bushes outside, with keys tucked into stockings.

Stockings must be stuffed beyond recognition.

Once the domain of three oranges and an apple, stockings have become a major drain on the Christmas budget. Fruit still plays a role, but it is not to be consumed, nor is the child expected to care about it. Rather, large and stubborn citrus fruits are inserted into the stocking to create a five-second lapse for the flash to recharge between "Look at the camera and show Mommy and Daddy how happy you are to see your Add-A-Pearl grow" and "Look at the camera and show Mommy and Daddy how happy you are that Santa left you a luncheon-size salad fork in your silver pattern."

Each year, the Humane Society publicizes the tragic abandonment of Christmas puppies and kittens. Far more tragic are the thousands of Add-A-Pearl strands left snaggletoothed and abandoned by grandparents and godparents who promised to contribute a pearl for each special occasion. This is where Santa comes in via the parents' rotating account at the jewelers, reaching ever closer each year to that ultimate goal of an eighteen-inch Mikimoto strand and service for eighteen.

That, in the South, is Christmas.

EPILOGUE

There's Got to Be a Morning After

A recent study showed that an alarming number of people in the Southern states report a condition known as postholiday depression. Symptoms of this condition include lethargy, lack of purpose, and a sense of emptiness.

To counter this empty feeling, it's important not to turn to pharmaceuticals or New Age cures.

Instead, look around with new eyes on Christmas morning. See what really matters. See the living room filled with the most important people in your life.

That won't necessarily cheer you up, so look a little closer. At your feet are mounds of gifts and neat stacks of carefully folded gift bags. Lack of purpose? Are you kidding? You have a regifting drawer to restock, and only 364 days to do it.

Acknowledgments

The team at MDi media group moved this book off start and into stockings. Much credit and thanks go to Don Davis, James Ellis, and especially to Tim Dozier for his collaboration as first-edition illustrator.

Then there's the Christmas miracle: Donna Adams at Little Professor Book Center in Homewood, Alabama, handed the book to William Morrow rep Michael Morris, who found an enthusiastic editor in Jennifer Pooley.

Many thanks to all involved, and to all a good night.